EAST OF AMERICA

EAST
OF
AMERICA

A SELECTION OF CAPE COD POEMS

EDITED BY JOHN V. HINSHAW

DRAWINGS BY RICHARD FISH

THE CHATHAM PRESS, INC., CHATHAM, MASSACHUSETTS

PS 595 C2 H5

ACKNOWLEDGMENTS

The editor wishes to thank the copyright owners for their permission to reprint poems from the works of the following poets:

CONRAD AIKEN: "Mayflower" (Part I) and "The Crystal" (Part II) are reprinted by permission of Brandt & Brandt, copyright © 1945, 1958 by Conrad Aiken from *Selected Poems*. Published by Oxford University Press, Inc.

ELIZABETH BISHOP: "Sandpiper" from *Questions of Travel* by Elizabeth Bishop, copyright © 1962 by Elizabeth Bishop, first appeared in the *New Yorker* Magazine. "Wading at Wellfleet" from *Poems North And South* by Elizabeth Bishop, copyright © 1940, 1946, 1947, 1948, 1949, 1951, 1952, 1955 by Elizabeth Bishop. Reprinted by permission of Farrar, Straus & Giroux, Inc.

JOHN PEALE BISHOP: "The 'Yankee Trader'" (Copyright © 1941 Charles Scribner's Sons) and "Nauset Sands" and "Cape Cod Graves" are reprinted with the permission of Charles Scribner's Sons from *The Collected Poems Of John Peale Bishop* edited by Allen Tate. Copyright © 1948 Charles Scribner's Sons.

CHARLES EDWARD EATON: "The Lighthouse," "The Fish Observed" and "Anchor" from *Shadows Of The Swimmer* by Charles Edward Eaton, copyright © 1951 by Charles Edward Eaton. Published by The Five Editions Press, New York. Reprinted by permission of Charles Edward Eaton.

THEODORE ENSLIN: "Ten Days From Work-In-Progress," "9/21/68" and "The Captain's Beard" are first published in this volume and are copyrighted © 1969 by Theodore Enslin.

PAUL GOODMAN: "Wellfleet Harbor (Manner Of Wordsworth)"; "From A High Dune" and "The Hurricane Of '54" reprinted with permission of The Macmillan Company from *The Lordly Hudson* by Paul Goodman. Copyright © by Paul Goodman 1961, 1962. "Wellfleet Harbor Wind Sun Space" Copyright © 1967 by Paul Goodman. Reprinted from *Hawkweed* by Paul Goodman by permission of Random House.

AMBROSE GORDON, JR.: "August At Wellfleet," copyright © 1960 by Carleton College, Northfield, Minnesota. Reprinted by permission of Ambrose Gordon, Jr.

JOHN HAY: "The Herring-Run" and "Man Of The Sea" from *A Private History* by John Hay, copyright © 1943, 1945, 1946, 1947 by John Hay. "Between The Tides" from *Wake*, copyright © 1951 by Wake Editions, Inc. "Town Meeting" from *New Poems By American Poets*

FOREWORD

Conrad Aiken, who once studied at Harvard under George Santayana, was asked recently if he had been influenced by his teacher. "Yes," replied Mr. Aiken, "I had from him the notion that the best poetry has to have a world view."

In seeking poems for *East of America* this statement has been uppermost in my mind and has formed the basis upon which the final selection was made. In a few poems, notably those of Conrad Aiken and Theodore Enslin, the setting is incidental to the theme. In most of them Cape Cod images provide a foundation or focal point upon which the poet has expressed a wider "world view." Santayana's "Cape Cod" is one of the finest examples of such poetry.

The poems are presented in order by birth dates of the poets, thus giving *East of America* a chronological pattern extending from Santayana at the turn of the century to Mary Oliver whose poems were written during the past few years. Brief biographical notes explaining the poets' associations with Cape Cod will be found at the end of the book.

The response from poets, poetry editors and others to requests for Cape Cod poems or suggestions as to where to find such poetry has been extremely gratifying. I am greatly indebted to these individuals who made *East of America* possible, and hope they will enjoy the book as much as I have enjoyed compiling it.

John V. Hinshaw
March, 1969

CONTENTS

CAPE COD

The low sandy beach and the thin scrub pine,
The wide reach of bay and the long sky line,—
    O, I am far from home!

The salt, salt smell of the thick sea air,
And the smooth round stones that the ebbtides wear,—
    When will the good ship come?

The wretched stumps all charred and burned,
And the deep soft rut where the cartwheel turned,—
    Why is the world so old?

The lapping wave, and the broad gray sky
Where the cawing crows and the slow gulls fly,—
    Where are the dead untold?

The thin, slant willows by the flooded bog,
The huge stranded hulk and the floating log,—
    Sorrow with life began!

And among the dark pines, and along the flat shore,
O the wind, and the wind, for evermore!
    What will become of man?

George Santayana

THE COD-FISHER

Where leap the long Atlantic swells
In foam-streaked stretch of hill and dale,
Where shrill the north-wind demon yells,
And flings the spindrift down the gale;
Where, beaten 'gainst the bending mast,
The frozen raindrop clings and cleaves,
With steadfast front for calm or blast
His battered schooner rocks and heaves.

> *To some the gain, to some the loss,*
> *To each the chance, the risk, the fight:*
> *For men must die that men may live—*
> *Lord, may we steer our course aright.*

The dripping deck beneath him reels,
The flooded scuppers spout the brine;
He heeds them not, he only feels
The tugging of a tightened line.
The grim white sea-fog o'er him throws
Its clammy curtain, damp and cold;
He minds it not—his work he knows,
'T is but to fill an empty hold.

Oft, driven through the night's blind wrack,
He feels the dread berg's ghastly breath,
Or hears draw nigh through walls of black
A throbbing engine chanting death;
But with a calm, unwrinkled brow
He fronts them, grim and undismayed,
For storm and ice and liner's bow—
These are but chances of the trade.

Yet well he knows—where'er it be,
On low Cape Cod or bluff Cape Ann—
With straining eyes that search the sea
A watching woman waits her man:
He knows it, and his love is deep,
But work is work, and bread is bread,
And though men drown and women weep
The hungry thousands must be fed.

To some the gain, to some the loss,
To each his chance, the game with Fate:
For men must die that men may live—
Dear Lord, be kind to those who wait.

Joseph Lincoln

THE SURF ALONG THE SHORE

Ye children of the mountain, sing of your craggy peaks,
Your valleys forest laden, your cliffs where Echo speaks;
And ye, who by the prairies your childhood's joys have seen,
Sing of your waving grasses, your velvet miles of green:
But when my memory wanders down to the dear old home
I hear, amid my dreaming, the seething of the foam,
The wet wind through the pine trees, the sobbing crash and
    roar,
The mighty surge and thunder of the surf along the shore.

I see upon the sand-dunes the beach-grass sway and swing,
I see the whirling sea-birds sweep by on graceful wing,
I see the silver breakers leap high on shoal and bar,
And hear the bell-buoy tolling his lonely note afar.
The green salt-meadows fling me their salty, sweet perfume,
I hear, through miles of dimness, the watchful fog-horn boom;
Once more, beneath the blackness of night's great roof-tree
    high,
The wild geese chant their marches athwart the arching sky.

The dear old Cape! I love it! I love its hills of sand,
The sea-wind singing o'er it, the seaweed on its strand;
The bright blue ocean 'round it, the clear blue sky o'erhead;
The fishing boats, the dripping nets, the white sails filled and
    spread;—
For each heart has its picture, and each its own home song,
The sights and sounds which move it when Youth's fair
    memories throng;
And when, down dreamland pathways, a boy, I stroll once
    more,
I hear the mighty music of the surf along the shore.

Joseph Lincoln

LITTLE BARE FEET

Little bare feet, sunburned and brown,
Patterin', patterin' up and down,
Dancin' over the kitchen floor,
Light as the foam-flakes on the shore,—
Right on the go from morn till late,
From the garden path ter the old front gate,—
There hain't no music ter me so sweet
As the patterin' sound of them little bare feet.

When I mend my nets by the foamin' sea,
Them little bare feet trot there with me,
And a shrill little voice I love 'll say:
"Dran'pa, spin me a yarn ter-day."
And I know when my dory comes ter land
There's a spry little form somewheres on hand;
And the very fust sound my ears 'll meet
Is the welcomin' run of them little bare feet.

Oh, little bare feet! how deep you've pressed
Yer prints of love in my worn old breast!
And I sometimes think, when I come ter die,
'Twill be lonesome-like in the by and by;
That up in Heaven I'll long ter hear
That little child's voice, so sweet and clear;
That even there, on the golden street,
I'll miss the pat of them little bare feet.

Joseph Lincoln

AT THE HELM

Beneath an endless midnight set alone
There looms a helmsman at a lonely wheel;
Aloofness works into his very bone
While down the sky the constellations steal;
His fellows sleep; the sails reach, starry-still,
Complete with steady wind; the whispering sea
Makes silence larger than itself can be:
Nor is it but a mortal ship he's sailing . . .
Before the dawn begins with heaven's paling
Somehow the helmsman knows another's Will,
Somehow perceives a cargo that's consigned
To no known port with mortal wharfage lined:
He sunders stars; he cleaves infinity,
And turns the helm unto a port unknown.

Harry Kemp

ULTIMATE CHALLENGE

Especially if their lading be a dream
Ships must go lonely if they'd voyage far;
Felling the up-surge, through each brace and beam.
Of fuming oceans; top and shrouded spar
Set to the following of a single star!—
There's no safe compass, when the hidden gleam
Sits behind clouds, and when blind tempests stream,
Except the guiding laurels faith would wear!
There often bide black gales and bursting beams,
And sails that fly in rags from broken spars:
There are no charts for ships that follow dreams
And crowd up sails against the beckoning stars:
Don't sign aboard—unless you're certain you
Can dare a wreck, and deem it glory, too!

Harry Kemp

16

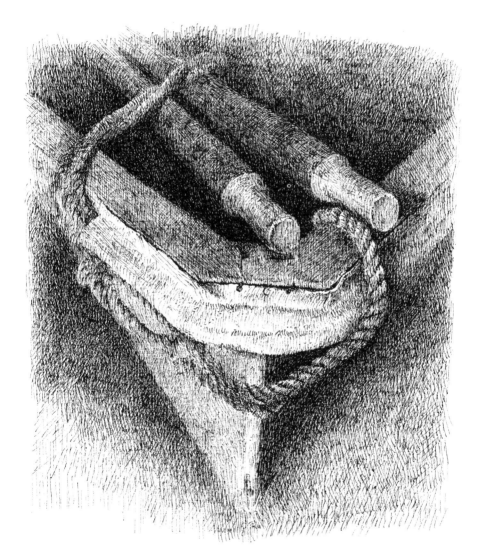

MAYFLOWER

Part I

Listen: the ancient voices hail us from the farther shore:
now, more than ever, in the New England spring,
we hear from the sea once more
the ghostly leave-takings, the hawser falling, the anchor
    weighing,
cries and farewells, the weeping on the quayside, and the
    praying:
and the devout fathers, with no thought to fail,
westward to unknown waters set joyless sail,
and at length, 'by God's providence,' 'by break of day espied
land, which we deemed to be Cape Cod.'
'It caused us to rejoice together and praise God,
seeing so goodly a land, and wooded to the brink of the sea.'
And still we share that providential tide,
the pleasant bay, wooded on every side
with 'oaks, pines, juniper, sassafras,' and the wild fowl rising
in clouds and numbers past surmising.
Yes: the ancient voices speak once more,
as spring, praised then by Will and Ben,
winds up our country clock again:
their spring, still living, now
when caterpillars tent the bough,
and seagulls speak
over the ale-wives running in Payne Creek.
The lyre-tree, seven-branched, the ancient plum, has cast
her sterile bloom, and the soft skin is cast
to glisten on the broken wall,
where the new snake sleeps in altered light;
and before sun-up, and late at night,
the pinkwinks shrill, the pinkwinks trill,
crying from the bog's edge to lost Sheepfold Hill.
Spring, spring, spring, spring, they cry,
water voice and reed voice,
spring, spring, spring, spring, they rejoice,
we who never die, never die!
But already the mayflower on the side hill is brown and dry,
Dry Hill is dry, the bog is drained,

and although for weeks it has not rained,
and the quick plough breaks dust,
yet towards summer the golden-rod and wormwood thrust.
The woodchuck is in the peas. And on his log,
the whip-poor-will shrieks and thumps in the bright May-
    morning fog.

Three hundred years from Will and Ben,
and the crab-apple sage at Hawthornden;
and now they wind our country clock again,
themselves, whose will it was that wound it then.
Three hundred years of snow and change,
the Mermaid voices growing lost and strange;
heard at first clearly on this yellow sand,
ghost voices, shadow of ghost and whisper of ghost,
haunting us briefly in the bright and savage land,
heard in the sea-roar, then sunk in silence, lost.
Yet not lost wholly:
in deed, in charter, and in covenant sweetly kept,
in laws and ordinances, in the Quaker's Thee and Thou,
in the grave rites of birth and death, the marriage vow,
and the ballad's melancholy.
Sung by the driftwood fire or behind the plough,
in the summer-kitchen to the warm cricket-song,
sung at maying, sung at haying,
shouted at husking to the fiddle's playing,
murmured to the cradle's rocking,
and the wheel humming, the treadle knocking.
And in the names kept too: sorrel and purslane,
ground-ivy, catnip, elecampane,
burdock and spurge, and sultry tansy,
woad-waxen, and the johnny-jump-up pansy.
Yet even so, though in the observance kept,
here most of all where first our fathers stept,
was something of the spirit that became idle, and at last
lost all that love; and heard no more
the voices singing from a distant shore.
Intricately, into the present, sank the past:
or, dreaming only of the future, slept.

Conrad Aiken

THE CRYSTAL

Part II

Six o'clock, here, in the western world, a west
unknown to sailor Kolaios, or the porters of Tartessus.
Stony Brook ferries its fins to the sea. Four bells
sing now in the fisherman's lighted cabin
above the brass binnacle and the floating compass.
Six o'clock in the cone of the Equinox, the bells
echo over mud-flats, sift through the nets
where mackerel flap and flash in the pools,
and over the oyster-beds, the shells of the razor-fish,
borne inland, to be echoed again
by the austere bell in the puritan steeple.
At seven, in the ancient farmhouse,
cocktails sparkle on the tray, the careful answer
succeeds the casual question, a reasoned dishevelment
ruffling quietly the day's or the hour's issue.
Our names, those we were born with,
or those we were not born with, since all are born nameless,
become the material, or the figment, if we wish,
of which to weave, and then unweave, ourselves.
Our lives, those we inherited, of which
none can claim ownership in fee simple, but only
a tenant's lease, of unpredictable duration,
rented houses from which have already departed perhaps
those others, our other selves, the children:
ourselves in these on our way beyond death
to become the undying succession of inheritors:
these and other aspects of the immortal moment
glow into consciousness for laughter or tears,
an instant of sympathy or misunderstanding, an exchange
of human touch or tact, or agreement, soon silent.

And here, as in the silence, too, that follows,
like the peacock's eye of shadow round the lifted candle,
is the tacit acceptance of death. We invoke,
and what is life but an invocation,
the shore beyond the vortex, the light beyond the dark,
the number beneath the name. We shall not be here
to pour the bright cocktails, while we listen
to the throb of migrant wings in the night air,
the chorus of departing voices, the bells from the bay;
and yet, brother Pythagoras, like you,
who still set your sail this night to the west,
we too shall be held so. After our deaths
we too shall be held so. And thus, brought together.

Conrad Aiken

NAUSET SANDS

Elude the dunes! By sunken pace
Through struggling sands,
Patched by the panting beach grass, come
To the long coast arrayed by sea-piled storms.

The north stands
Dissolute sands,
Sea-borne bulwarks against the sea.

South is an unlimited strand,
A waste of noon
Paced by no shadow.

And here the lonely man may stride
Unmeasured by the beach,
Strip, run and plunge
Through inborn sunburnt spray,
Then glistening stretch
Where in the destroying radiance
Of the aroused day
No shell survives. An imagined east
The sea! And all America is west!
And here at last a naked man may rest
Undaunted by the ancestral quest
As though it had not been,
In azure assumption of pure space
Untortured by the undaunted dream,
An hour stay, unshadowed of the sun,
And this the first as now the ultimate coast.

II

Domain that has no confines but in light,
Destroying space! Brute blue of noon now glared
Its death upon me. I saw them on their coast,
Their hearts as big with winds as though they had been sails,
And all their purpose prows turned into the sun.
Undream their doing. Lie down! Lie down!
The sea returns upon an instant and all their voyages
End at last in a bare body on the sand.
Into the world naked I came
And now once more lie naked to the sky.

John Peale Bishop

CAPE COD GRAVES

Sea dunes, sand waves
That shape the shudder of the winds,
These are the true accumulations,
As the sea, that old trickster, is the true grave.

Look at the tumbling stones on the old mounds!
Titles to graves. Each has a name.
But go down into the ground,
Deep, deep, deep. The sea has the bones.

At seadawn the surge sang
And all day the sea brought what day sought.
At dusk the sea surged. And the sea sang
A doom's dream of drowned men's bones.

Scrub pine, sand pine,
Twisted by the gale's tang, tough
In a cloud, elude no storm. Pines hold
The harried hollows behind the dunes.

Standing at land's end, these are the trees,
These are the trees to look upon,
And the sea, the sea, that receives a man
And with one wave washes away the name.

The grave is not a door through which to escape
The body of this death
When bare age has scraped all memory from bone.
The grave is a squall.

When song surged, the sea sang
Its own change. Hungry for land,
Hastening spawn, distributing wrack,
The sea's sound was a joy of fear.

Cir. 1942   *John Peale Bishop*

THE 'YANKEE TRADER'

An old sofa has been abandoned
At the *Yankee Trader*, an old sofa
Has been left out in the snow.

Slightly lopsided, it still proposes
With its faded roses positions for courtships
Proper and poised against the snow.

With its sodden roses under the snow
And its stiff scrolls, the sofa recovers
The stiffer backs and the sobbing postures:

A coffin treading on legs through doors,
A family fading into the snow.
The doors are closed on the *Yankee Trader*.

An old sofa, coldly abandoned,
Might still support, more patient than lovers,
The fall of snow on its final roses,

Outstaying men, may still withstand
Eternal fault in the falling elements,
A stiff wind and the approaching snow.

1940   *John Peale Bishop*

MEMORY OF CAPE COD

The wind in the ash-tree sounds like surf on the shore at Truro.
I will shut my eyes . . . hush, be still with your silly bleating,
    sheep on Shillingstone Hill . . .

They said: Come along! They said: Leave your pebbles on the
    sand and come along, it's long after sunset!
The mosquitoes will be thick in the pine-woods along by Long
    Nook, the wind's died down!
They said: Leave your pebbles on the sand, and your shells, too,
    and come along, we'll find you another beach like the beach
    at Truro.

Let me listen to wind in the ash . . . it sounds like surf on the
    shore.

Edna St. Vincent Millay

PROVINCETOWN

We never from the barren down,
    Beneath the silver lucent breast
Of drifting plume, gazed out to drown
    Where daylight whitens to the west.

Here never in this place I knew
    Such beauty by your side, such peace—
These skies that brightening imbue
    With dawn's delight the day's release.

Only, upon the barren beach,
    Beside the gray egg of a gull,
With that fixed look and fervent speech,
    You stopped and called it beautiful.

Lone as the voice that sped the word!—
    Gray-green as eyes that ate its round!—
The desert dropping of a bird,
    Bare-bedded in the sandy ground.

To-night, where clouds like foam are blown,
    I ride alone the surf of light—
As—even by my side—alone,
    That stony beauty burned your sight.

Edmund Wilson

PROVINCETOWN, 1936

Fat-pronged starfish, oyster-fed,
That slow on spirit fingers slide;
Snails in plump blue folds that spread
Purple feet below the tide;

Crabs that, humped in stolen homes,
Fence from doors they cannot lock;
Polyps budded pink, like wombs,
Filamented to the rock;

Sand-dabs sandside up in pools,
That slip in bat-flights from the hand;
Tiny mackerel trapped in twinkling schools;
The little silver eels that dive into the sand—

Mussels with broken hinges, sea crabs lopped
Of legs, black razor-clams split double, dried
Sea-dollars, limpets chivied loose and dropped
Like stranded dories rolling on their side:

They lose their juice and stiffen in the sun:
The tide that shrinks has shed them like a scurf;
The tide that floods will stir with waves that stun
Frail shapes that crush before the faintest surf.

Edmund Wilson

CAPE COD

Here where your blue bay's hook is half begun,
    I find you fled on those mad rounds you make—
    As if with sleepless demons on your track,
Yet lodging with the daughters of the sun—
Pursuing still that high romantic mood
    Through flight from love to love, from friend to friend;
    While she who dwells there sovereign to the end
Draws now her final strength from solitude.

—Yes, moored in a shadowy room I have seen that shape—
    Who once by sleepless winds herself was sped—
        She haunts me here in mind's and time's despite—
The last gray clouds and pale gold of the Cape—
    The scent of sweet-fern crushed beneath my tread,
        As once I smelt it through the smothered night.

—And you who faint at either's hard expense;
    Who idle and in exile almost grow
    That comfortable personage you show—
Almost persuaded by your own pretense—
Bred to one world and baffled by this other,
    Too poor for pride, too courtly for compliance—
    Did you and I once frame a late defiance
Against that world of desk and death, together?

—Old friend, fine poet—those romantic skies
    Have fallen—shall we harvest ray or flake?—
The very language of that vision lies.
    Yet who for doubt, for danger, may not quake—
Though all the darkness throng behind his eyes—
    Imagining a world his words must make?

Edmund Wilson

THINKING OF FRIENDS WHO ARE
WINTERING ON CAPE COD

For Charles and Deborah Philbrick

I like a cold beach on a gray day. Remember
Me in November and December
When the Cape's taut arm springs bicep-bulged
Against the tides which it indulged
In the—dreamed was it?—summer of your early stay,
But now against tides ominous with spray:
How they roar in with that boom-bumbling stumbling
As if they would never halt—and no less humbling
Their hurricane-seethed screech, withdrawing;
Is there rain in your eyes or spindrift yawing
While spinnaker clouds press the far flatted sea?

When you walk the hardened dunes, remember me
As an out-of-season lover, if you will,
Where what compass grass wrote rounds stiff and still
And carved, if anything can be carved, in sand;
And amidst the cohabit odors of marshes inland
With salt gust of beach which breathes wet stones,
Dead starfish, blacked seaweed, clamshells, fishbones;
When you get, hoping for menace, that human wish
The dark day be darker before night makes its finish—
Even unseen flickers of snow, promise of storm;
And when you go indoors and begin to be warm.

Winfield Townley Scott

THE SPOOL AND THE LIGHTHOUSE

I saw my gone years turning in the sky—
Brightly away from me and then returning
Returning with vast shapes of mist: I see
Far to the south the sun's bafflement.

Spool of my gathering spawn a patient wheel
Winding my seasons. But the world turns two ways
Therefore, too, the lighthouse that swings
Round into dark, round into dark, round . . .

Always going. The beam of time spins
A halo, and what was dark on earth
Is dark; but what was bright recedes
Always going. And evening tall in the north.

Winfield Townley Scott

WELLFLEET HARBOR WIND SUN SPACE

North Wind across the dunes and bays,
sweep away hatred, be praise.
    Hatred has been half of me
    but it's boring, praise is free.

Hot Sun, who makes earth green and tan,
give heat and color to this man.
    The blank morose where I have been
    is dull, I long for tan and green.

Great Spaces of the bays and islands
and ocean crashing down from the horizon,
    without effort here you are,
    make me be here who have been far.

I am a native, on my home
rocks of the world I play like foam,
    my quick spirit gives delight
    and little children send me soaring like a kite.

Paul Goodman

WELLFLEET HARBOR
(MANNER OF WORDSWORTH)

I unbelieving saw a white spire far
    on the blue bay and thought I heard its bell,
    but veering in the wind it was a bright sail
instantaneously triangular.
        Again the bell jangled far and clear
        across the water to my astonished ear.

That white sail like a comma in the long
    proposition of the blue bay sped
    toward the bold headland that was blanketed
with furze and dune. I followed where she swung
        around the cape and like a period
        ended, and it was silent where I stood.

Paul Goodman

33

FROM A HIGH DUNE

Still—I light my pipe unshielded
quiet—I can hear the Boston mail
immense immense—the bathers bob
in the fringes of the globe-encircling sea.

The cannon of the range at Nauset
are thundering at the blue blinding day.
The rollers are rolling evenly in
from a hurricane four hundred miles away.

Paul Goodman

THE HURRICANE OF '54

The hurricane of '54
that knocked the spire off Old North Church
no damage did to me and mine
for the house that Williams built
and many friends drove nails
houselikely sheltered us
as at the streaming windows
we saw bay flood the meadow
dunes fly up in clouds
the fishing-fleet destroyed
but the elastic pines
wrestle the winds and win.
The storm was circular,
first from the east the blow
sought us out, it blasted
our south as laughing sun
leaked through the wild spray,
for hours west wall bore it,
as evening fell departed
the gentle gale from the north.
The barometer rose, the vortex
has left the kitchen, sea-gulls
are soaring from Blackfish Creek,
cars are roaring to Wellfleet,
the woods are pruned, the world
is washed, and the townspeople
will talk of nothing else forever,
a bore for years to come.
For young folk talk about animals
but old folk like to dwell
minutely on disasters.

Paul Goodman

SANDPIPER

The roaring alongside he takes for granted,
and that every so often the world is bound to shake.
He runs, he runs to the south, finical, awkward,
in a state of controlled panic, a student of Blake.

The beach hisses like fat. On his left, a sheet
of interrupting water comes and goes
and glazes over his dark and brittle feet.
He runs, he runs straight through it, watching his toes.

—Watching, rather, the spaces of sand between them,
where (no detail too small) the Atlantic drains
rapidly backwards and downwards. As he runs,
he stares at the dragging grains.

The world is a mist. And then the world is
minute and vast and clear. The tide
is higher or lower. He couldn't tell you which.
His beak is focussed; he is preoccupied,

looking for something, something, something.
Poor bird, he is obsessed!
The millions of grains are black, white, tan, and gray,
mixed with quartz grains, rose and amethyst.

Elizabeth Bishop

WADING IN WELLFLEET

In one of the Assyrian wars
a chariot first saw the light
that bore sharp blades around its wheels.

That chariot from Assyria
went rolling down mechanically
to take the warriors by the heels.

A thousand warriors in the sea
could not consider such a war
as that the sea itself contrives

but hasn't put in action yet.
This morning's glitterings reveal
the sea is 'all a case of knives.'

Lying so close, they catch the sun,
the spokes directed at the shin.
The chariot front is blue and great.

The war rests wholly with the waves:
they try revolving, but the wheels
give way; they will not bear the weight.

Elizabeth Bishop

THE HERRING-RUN

By day and night, out of the law of leaden tides,
Migration and death through the inland gauntlet, where the
    gulls,
Like vultures hunting high air of dying, circle and scream.

The pale blind fish, in millions, move from the ocean walls—
Salt gulfs and dark devouring—to fight the sun,
In the shallow waters crystal to a hunter's eye.

On the stream bed flowing, their sinuous shadows on the sand,
They waver backward with the weeds; processional
In tide and stars, pulsed forward by the drums of time.

Soft in the currents, spineless as the water's flow;
And then they leap! Taut daring at the wires, the high
And highest trial; their wounds; their white resplendent scales!

The male and female, power and spawn, rocket through rage
Of rocks, black storms and flailing torrents on their flesh,
To meet the silent lakes, perfection's morning womb.

They die shining. The splash of moons and golden lust
Of rivers loads the nets, as they protest and praise,
In the last quick leaps and running of their great desire.

John Hay

BETWEEN THE TIDES

That we should be there was an accident.
That we together, caught between the tides,
Should not have seen, was negligent,
The inland sands being the inland way.

But in our dereliction we could find
No other danger than the light. The light
Of day to splintered waters struck us blind;
The sea glass breaking as it formed again;

And there was no way out but to be lost,
Blind only in that brightness, at a point
Of artifice, where green and sapphire crossed
Through crucibles above the vanished sands,

Blowing to glass, as delicate as spray,
And splendid as the fires of the tide.
Our inland bodies, outcast in the way
Of light, were drawn into ascendancy,

Fired with waters in a sacrifice,
Between the striking of the sea and sky.
They were not less than glass in artifice,
To break and form again; not less than love.

John Hay

TOWN MEETING

The Meeting's in order. What's coming? What's to come?
The health officer says death. The carpenter
Says everything is shipshape. The minister
Says God—we try to say it too, like that,
But a frog croaks in our throats. Then nobody speaks
For weeks. Isn't there something we mean to say?
Is the coming never to be come to? Speak!
Mr. Moderator, don't hold him down—the spark,
The star, the old, love-flinted animal.
Don't stop him saying what we knew before we came.

John Hay

MAN OF THE SEA

Cold and sonorous still, the sea broke out,
And led me from my derelict dismay.
It stood me on the sand, throwing its white
Commandments at my ribs until I sang.

That music I remembered—past my stay
In wars and cardboard towns. The tides were sprung
With song, which followed me until I found
My head was ringing like the strident birds.

I traced the sea's green lip, where sandpipers
Were cutting veins and flowers in the sand.
I heard them flitter off, through walls of spray,
And felt heir bones in timbre to the waves.

Where sea grass flicked meridians, I danced.
I turned my head to armories of shells;
And made a crown of salt and cloth of wind,
To fit myself for sundowns choked with clouds.

But then I ran and took my liberty.
I tore the tide and broke the waves; while terns
Were diving down the sky, in silver shafts,
To fall upon that sounding royalty.

John Hay

ANCHOR

On the beach, rusty, half-hidden, locked deep
In a belly mound of sand,
An anchor pierces down, upright,
Strong enough with the wind for a rope to keep
The sky from skittering off the land.
Looking deep-down-earth, only half in light,
Male in its metalness, unmistakably man-made,
It offers to your hand the gaping ring that held the fat rope
    girth.
When you strain to lift it, the sinews of your arm twisting in a
    tawny braid,
The flukes hold, and you have struck a mooring in the earth.

Charles Edward Eaton

THE FISH OBSERVED

He gasps in the sand before the still life in him wins,
Fighting the effect, fighting the cause as well, for that matter:
If he doesn't become a painting, he may end up in tins.

He is the spokesman for those who would not be arranged.
He made the mistake of rising to the bait, the dream of plenty,
And felt remorse hemorrhage through his hooked head—an
    undersea Utopia expunged.

Panting, streaming blood, mythical as a heart,
He has the totally denuding experience of being pitilessly
    observed
And a glaze comes into his eyes like milk glass buttons on a
    sequined shirt.

All blue and silver shadow jellied in the plate, sliced lemon, and
    a knife—
The saving grace is that these dead pieces may be strangely
    beautiful:
What sang back and forth along the line if it were not postulates
    in strife?

There is penitence in the look of the scarred but loving eye
Which has itself hung more than once upon a hook,
Observed how little it could do and what it might blindly try.

Will we not always, then, detect a covert spasm
In the thing accounted for, ruthlessly secured, the
    cut-and-dried,
As if the eye supplies the garden of the sea for this uncovered
    rhizome?

Charles Edward Eaton

THE LIGHTHOUSE

Upon this florid coast a lighthouse turns
Its compact spiral to a point of view;
Hard, white, it soars between the wood that burns,
Green-smouldering, and sea of violent blue.

A mastery, spired in stone, from this look-out
Impends the ground. Aloft the arduous stair
We track the whale whose silver phantom-spout
Is shadow of a tower crumbling in the air.

We stay until the mammoth wake is gone—
On the stairs descending in forever,
Through close-packed darkness wound and drawn,
Still the whiteness soars above our fever.

Height-rapt, we stand too level with the waves,
Shun the corpulent blue's decaying gleam;
When tide sucks out the force that flowing gives,
The world is drained of its flamboyant dream.

Once more we scan the shadow-furling dome
And shudder when the clamorous gulls alight
As though the walls might fall with thundering boom
And blanch a vast abyss across the night.

But shaft, unseen, strikes force in concentrate—
With sea and wood, jet-knit, the body blind—
The light, delved intricate-obscure by fate,
Probes through the dark and will not be confined.

Charles Edward Eaton

AUGUST AT WELLFLEET

Barnacles in the branches, while underfoot
The slop of the eternal sea against a stone
Possessed the deckchair dallier's mind—his weary eyes,
Goggled and fabulous, revolving inward find
After this morning's game of chess, the clams, a can of ale
The flux and reflux of a summer seaside afternoon.

And so he drops off, drifts far away . . .
To sink full fathom five, and swirl
Untented in the wide whale's acre, where
All living movement quickens as the light how gently,
Softly and silently, thickens and dims
Merging into the boom of a sunken surf.

                          But now
From somewhere near at hand (behold!) thin shadows
Of foundered ships and seabells call and beckon
Him, pale loiterer of the bottom, who caught up among
The swaying tentacles of a giant squid, hears,
Or thinks he hears,
"Gray human oyster, swing your partner, come!"
He struggles, weighted down, to join the dance.

He vaguely knows this music stretched about him
Was never of the spheres, nor even
A hornpipe skirled in Davy Jones's locker.
The horns were not the wreathed horns of Triton—
Of Buick rather, M.G., Packard, Chevrolet,
His daughter homebound with a dozen beaux or brother.
And knows, importantly, that cocktails will await him
With the Alice Murphys or the Isabella Joneses,
To be followed by a drive, live lobsters, and a full shore dinner.

Ambrose Gordon, Jr.

THE SALT GARDEN

for S.M.S.

I

A good house, and ground whereon
With an amateur's toil
Both lawn and garden have been won
From a difficult, shallow soil
That, now inland, was once the shore
And once, maybe, the ocean floor.
Much patience, and some sweat,
Have made the garden green,
An even green the lawn.
Turnip and bean and violet
In a decent order set,
Grow, flourish and are gone;
Even the ruins of stalk and shell,
The vine when it goes brown,
Look civil and die well.
Sometimes in the late afternoon
I sit out with my wife,
Watching the work that we have done
Bend in the salt wind,
And think that here our life
Might be a long and happy one;
Though restless over the sand
The ocean's wrinkled green
Maneuvers in its sleep,
And I despise what I had planned,
Every work of the hand,
For what can man keep?

II

Restless, rising at dawn,
I saw the great gull come from the mist
To stand upon the lawn.
And there he shook his savage wing
To quiet, and stood like a high priest
Bird-masked, mantled in grey.

Before his fierce austerity
My thought bowed down, imagining
The wild sea lanes he wandered by
And the wild waters where he slept
Still as a candle in the crypt.
Noble, and not courteous,
He stared upon my green concerns,
Then, like a merchant prince
Come to some poor province,
Who, looking all about, discerns
No spice, no treasure house,
Nothing that can be made
Delightful to his haughty trade,
And so spreads out his sail,
Leaving to savage men
Their miserable regimen;
So did he rise, making a gale
About him by his wings,
And fought his huge freight into air
And vanished seaward with a cry—
A strange tongue but the tone clear.
He faded from my troubled eye
There where the ghostly sun
Came from the mist.
                  When he was gone
I turned back to the house
And thought of wife, of child,
And of my garden and my lawn
Serene in the wet dawn;
And thought that image of the wild
Wave where it beats the air
Had come, brutal, mysterious,
To teach the tenant gardener,
Green fellow of this paradise,
Where his salt dream lies.

Howard Nemerov

SHELLS

You pick one up along the shore.
It is empty and light and dry,
And leaves a powdery chalk on your hands.

The life that made it is gone out.
That is what is meant when people say,
"A hollow shell," "a shell of his former self,"

Failing to take into account
The vital waste in composition
With the beauty of the ruined remainder

Which is no use to anyone,
Of course, unless as decoration:
A Souvenir of Sunset Beach, etc.

Its form is only cryptically
Instructive, if at all: it winds
Like generality, from nothing to nothing

By means of nothing but itself.
It is a stairway going nowhere,
Our precious emblem of the steep ascent,

Perhaps, beginning at a point
And opening to infinity,
Or the other way, if you want it the other way.

Inside it, also, there is nothing
Except the obedient sound of waters
Beat by your Mediterranean, classic heart

In bloody tides as long as breath,
Bringing by turns the ebb and flood
Upon the ruining house of histories,

Whose whitening stones, in Africa,
Bake dry and blow away, in Athens,
In Rome, abstract and instructive as chalk

When children scrawl the blackboard full
Of wild spirals every which way,
To be erased with chalk dust, then with water.

Howard Nemerov

THE GULLS

I know them at their worst, when by the shore
They raise the screaming practice of their peace,
Disputing fish and floating garbage or
Scraps of stale bread thrown by a child. In this,
Even, they flash with senseless beauty more
Than I believed—sweet are their bitter cries,
As their fierce eyes are sweet; in their mere greed
Is grace, as they fall splendidly to feed.

And sometimes I have seen them as they glide
Mysterious upon a morning sea
Ghostly with mist, or when they ride
White water or the shattered wind, while we
Work at a wooden oar and huddle inside
Our shallow hull against the sea-torn spray;
And there they brutally are emblems of
Soul's courage, summoners to a broken love.

Courage is always brutal, for it is
The bitter tooth fastens the soul to God
Unknowing and unwilling, but as a vise
Not to be torn away. In the great crowd,
Because it gathers from such empty skies,
Each eye is arrogant and each voice loud
With angry lust; while alone each bird must be
Dispassionate above a hollow sea.

White wanderers, sky-bearers from the wide
Rage of the waters! so may your moving wings
Defend you from the kingdom of the tide
Whose sullen sway beneath your journeyings

Wrinkles like death, so may your flying pride
Keep you in danger—bless the song that sings
Of mortal courage; bless it with your form
Compassed in calm amid the cloud-white storm.

Howard Nemerov

50

WELLFLEET: THE HOUSE

Roof overwoven by a soft tussle of leaves,
The walls awave with sumac shadow, lilac
Lofts and falls in the yard, and the house believes
It's guarded, garlanded in a former while.

Here one cannot intrude, the stillness being
Lichenlike grown, a coating of quietudes;
The portraits dream themselves, they are done with seeing;
Rocker and teacart balance in iron moods.

Yet for the transient here is no offense,
Because at certain hours a wallowed light
Floods at the seaside windows, vague, intense,
And lays on all within a mending blight,

Making the kitchen silver blindly gleam,
The yellow floorboards swim, the dazzled clock
Boom with a buoy sound, the chambers seem
Alluvial as that champed and glittering rock

The sea strokes up to fashion dune and beach
In strew by strew, and year by hundred years.
One is at home here. Nowhere in ocean's reach
Can time have any foreignness or fears.

Richard Wilbur

AT THE WELLFLEET HISTORICAL SOCIETY, DURING A MODERATE TEMPEST

We slammed in out of the summer storm,
Shook, dripped, squeezed hair and hushed the children;
Then started to circle the past, and peer in its corners.

There were sadirons sheer and solid as dreadnaughts,
Capstan-bars, quadrants, quilts and tin churns;
Daguerreotypes of the righteous buttonhooked tight
To the collar in beady-black strings of no nonsense,
Square wooden pattens for hoofs of obedient horses
Who hauled off the marshes the salt hay they lived on; the scoop
Of sloths' claws well fitted and polished, wood into wood,
That has outlived the cranberries here; the sparse-
Starred flags, the pillows patched and plumped for homing men,
Potato-mashers unchanged from my childhood, the
        gothic-backed potty-chair;
And the worn, humbling school-desk for midget seamen-to-be.

There were schoolbooks, paperknives slivered from transoms
Of famous wrecks; and scrimshawed tusks on which the boys
From Wellfleet School improved each idle and continent hour,
Scoring their fathers' votes, the whales and other objects of
        desire,
As they lolled in the doldrums of middle-Pacific, stinking
After the slaughters from which money rose like the soot.
Here a local gulliver's surgical kit for probing the whale
To deep death and grand transfigurations into corsets
And Bible-reading light; here models of four-finned schooners
That drew a full fathom through the yellowing charts and past
Lighthouses marking a land that has not survived its surveying.

And there was in the last upstairs corner the immaculate skull
Of the richly flinted and full-ribbed Pamet brave, a skull
Of such incised and settled shape, so right as to alert
All sculptors to the hopelessness of flesh-blurred heads.
This tenant of the land we buy and bully, tax, looks now
As though he'd smelled us coming, and it ate his nose away.

Down from his clean presence, past the stove-blacked safe
That housed a grandfather's haul and a few crisp clippings,
Back we came through all the dried produce of attics owned
By good granddaughters who thus outstripped the auctioneers,
Past the rusty flare-headed hatchets that hacked off disasters,

And out in this gale to the ocean at exercise under stiff skies.
Why am I so much involved with things I have never used,
Or seen except in the vast museums of memory?

Perhaps old notions like identity hide under dust,
And continuity's refreshed by swipes of spray;
History and the world's working brushed me with rust
Near both shores of Wellfleet, that loud and quiet day.

Charles Philbrick

THE BEACHING OF BENJAMIN

Out in the thatch-snatching, wig-lifting wind
Ran the rat-catching boy, the custodian of toads,
Detective of quahaugs, the butterflies' bane.
Benjamin Brighthair was running to run,
And drink up the wind in his halloween grin.
The master of monsters, who frightened old ladies
Out of their baggy big bathing suits, raced
Down prickly paths to the lap-lipping water,
Leaving his shadow behind in the sun.
He tore through the towels, and bounced over babies,
Splashing two yackety mothers in shallow,
And bashed in the water so hard the tide turned,
And boats began rocking all over the bay.
Then Benjamin Wethead shot shining from water,
Shaking and spouting and shouting to people
To plunge in the water and learn how to play.

Charles Philbrick

LOBSTERS AND GIN

Why can't all people live like the live great man—
Live despite, great because—the kind man I met
This summer who's known all those people and places
And times, and spun out all those poems that pluck
At the sensitive ear, and those other dark songs
That anchor fast under the shift and flow of the slick
On the reading-full mind?
                           O other eldering men,
Why have you put away all those canaries, brought home—
Accoladed, bifocalled and raised unto suburbs—the world's
Rancid bacon,
While Conrad Aiken
Can roll from his garden and quietly rollick,
Encouraging me? The answer is simple: we live on the fringes,
Desperately,
On lobsters and gin, and the thunder of unbuyable verse.

Charles Philbrick

DECLINE TO FALL

Supine in its dying fever, summer lies
Attended by the blossoms of dismay;
The birds of horror mount the moist skies,
And the children of regret go hustled away.

All that's left on this dried lawn alone
Is a great clean gull with a broken wing
Who parades his hurt as the sun goes down,
And stops to beak at his reddening wrong.

Sick summer, and the summer's gull,
Will cool and decay in tomorrow's air,
To the dry weep of petals, and the dull
Insistencies of the waves' despair.

These deaths presage the passage of green
In elaborate processions, yellow and red
As a gull's bill or gull's blood in the lawn
That will brown, be feathered white when dead.

But this is a camouflage death, all dressed
In forward beauty, borrowing blossoms' white
For its cerement, investing energy in rest,
Until the frozen summer lazes up from night.

Charles Philbrick

KENNINGS OF PRAISE

Shelf over shellfish, foundation for waves,
Greenhouse for seaweed and larder for terns,
Boat-floor and trapdoor for bodies of boatmen,
Skylighted ceiling for boat-handlers' prey,
Old innocent house of cold birth, quiet ruin:

Palette for whitecaps to clot with stiff foam,
Stippler of sun-glints and canvas for moonstroke,
Wood-wearer, stone-roller, sprayer of shells,
Sand-scroller, rock-draper, sculptor of cliffs,
Orchestra spread for the wind, and metrist of weather:

This easy sea that breeds and beggars epithets,
This water that always remembers, invents and forgets.

Charles Philbrick

TEN DAYS FROM WORK-IN-PROGRESS

Cahoon's Hollow
9/17/68

The wind is:
One direction,
the drift, another,
forming the clasp,
as
the problem is one
of survival—
that one comes thus far
wherever he may be
standing
                or
looking
                seaward.
Or that I am
                I
as I never was—
alive to remembrances
in going further.
There is a death in this—
but as the spirit lives.
Tossed in three crosswaves—
to come out again,
actual and alive,
but to have died there.
Surely.

The sound of ropes against
metal flagpoles
in the wind,
tuned to thirds, one place.
I had not thought to hear
or discover them.

In all this
            to know,
that with no commitments
I may come back again,
Wellfleet   and it is not return.
Walking and coveting,
but with no plan
save one:
to come back
time and another time—
and no return.
Whatever the impasse,
whatever impinges or impairs.
With no stake,
the return is possible.

Tied surely
to the madman and his horse,
his drunken rages dying
in the clatter of slow hooves.
It was to be expected.
to be known—
            a man
comes inquiring
            for my death
on a slow horse.

*   *   *   *   *

Things do not change in our times,
or in any lives.
I find now
            those same plants
I found
            twenty years ago—
in places
            I had thought
not to find.
            Unwithered.

It is merely myself
which ages.
                    Even that
adapts to thinkings—
what were once,
and no more ghosts.

Trying to complete
the page,
and an ocean swells.
Today is
            one of glassy sea
with groundswell,
                        as
yesterday with fog
and drifting wind
which bids a storm
ride in;
before that, surf
which calibrated dirty weather
far off.
Could I believe this,
or believe myself
scenting
salt decay?
Tense being is
no
      and
            no and
no.

Very good and very good,
that each thing in the teeth of death
should be enjoyed,
and known as such.
I walk out in the morning—
see what I have not seen,
rake in old oyster beds
I once knew—
            find what is contained
and little changed.

The red morning sun,
later, a coal in hand,
skimming and scouring the sea.
A feeling of health
in these,
       and clear
to be
    open
about it.

Day and a day,
and another one—
nights discounted.
How often—
and wherewith
I think of sea
and seasons
comparable only to themselves.
Lying back among
tide remnants
remembering:
the sea wind
from the south—
to follow the drift.
I do not capture much,
except what creates
in me the capture
yet
here I am.
Sense of capture—
sense of little
made and remade.
I did not return,
(but did, gainsaying it)
and what is here
was always and never—
a stranglehold on death,
which death
       has not,
          and
which death?

I think quickly of the skull
which frames my face
from inside—
as quickly
           try to forget it.
In such health
the dreams
which are uneasy dreams
with no such health
each night—
the complement of day.
I—
but I do not say it.

If I could talk to
you.
If you were here—
with me—
trails off
in the ninth wave.

Theodore Enslin

9/21/68

The little girl asks me
what I would do if I
found a pearl
in one of the oysters
I am opening,
              and I am
hard put to it.
She hopes I'll say
'make a million dollars,'
but she
accepts what I do say,
which is:
'I would give it to my wife.'
From there it is possible to go on to
the next oyster.

Theodore Enslin

THE CAPTAIN'S BEARD

Not that he will grow it
but that
        he has
top boat,
        and his wife
wouldn't mind
            if he did.

Theodore Enslin

THE CAPTAIN'S POND

In the dark world deep down in any sea
We guess what constancies of sway prevail.
Perhaps, if the Titanic and all wrecks
Sink gradually, some are sinking yet,
Still short of bottom, pendant, barnacled
To scratch the bulky backs of itching whales.
In this pond, no Atlantic, we feel sure
No ships repine unsettled; but who knows?
Its placid surface, at its most serene,
For which outsiders call it Crystal Lake,
Lets the most searching sun but slightly in,
Never revealing where or how belogged
Is last year's sunken rowboat. Bubbles rise
And break, to say this truly is Fresh Pond,
But give no evidence how deep their springs.
And the lengthiest diver, holding his best breath,
Sees only water, save a few small fish,
After the drop-off several yards from shore.

The Captain, then, was credulous when he came
To the long plank dock one August afternoon
And asked the children standing there entranced
What they were staring at.
                              "Linda's down there."
Nothing to see, nothing to be believed,
No special bubbles, just the bare remark,
But the Captain dove straight nine or ten feet down
To the muck—we all had touched it with our toes,
Holding our noses tight against the surge
Of the jumped water—and brought Linda back.
She had not long been under; thus, perhaps,
The casual wonder, not yet quite concern,
Of the children, watching where she'd come up next.
Taking turns, we pumped her body back to life,
Saved for some other death.

                          Later, near night,
We older children sat on that same dock
Looking into the lake, till someone said,
"Have other Lindas, drowned, fed the small fish?"
Fresh Pond seemed suddenly sinister and old
And Linda young and lucky, while a breeze
Brushed through high pines, wooing our sight away
From the unfathomed to the infinite,
From the deep waters to the deeper skies.
Then, looking nowhere, as the world grew dark
We drew together. No one said it out,
But implicitly, essentially, we felt
The Captain's credence as our constancy.
Had he not made things happen as they had
By refusing absolute sureness to his doubt
Of the children's words?
                          We were as sure of this
As we were certain, when we went to bed,
That each of us would sleep, and dream, and wake,
And see each other risen with the day,
Ready, like Linda, if she dared, to swim
On the safe surface of the Captain's pond.

                                   Thomas Whitbread

POCHET ISLAND

The ticks jumped on our legs as if we were dogs
As we walked to the beach through marsh-grass. Shaggily
We went, more shaggily each step. We stopped
Now and then to pick the ticks off. My dog Buff
Has similar, worse troubles, all the summer,
And has developed a stoic eye. We had
No such resource. We were glad to reach the sea.
After we swam, we walked back through more ticks
Picked off at intervals, to the house. I was
The outsider. The three others knew each other:
The husband, the wife, the husband's longtime friend.
Their talk was largely local. I sat in
Happily, though, since all three were nice, and I
Not unnice. We drank, ate, played Scrabble, then
Ran low on whiskey. We were on an island
Kerosene-lamped, a half-mile from the mainland, and
It was nine o'clock and raining. Therefore I
Volunteered, announced, insisted I would go
Provide. They got me into a sticky old
Two-piece rubber cement rainsuit, told me not
To go, gave me a flashlight, and I went.
Time was both fast and slow at once. I lost
An oar in the middle of the bay, said *no*
To panic, and with light and paddling found
It again. No trouble in returning. When
I got to the door with scotch and beer, she asked
Who I might be? what I was doing out
On a night like this? whether I knew the word
Of passage? was I friend or foe? My host
The husband said he had worried. His old friend
Approved the provisions. We played on into
The middle night, while a clock went tock and tick.

Next day, hungover, before breakfast of
Tomato juice, eggs, coffee, coffee, coffee,
I walked out in the rain-drenched grass down through
Rain-bearing bushes to the bay, and stood
Against a fresh gale, which made anything
Feel right. When I walked up and back, we were
Four friends. Such happenings give worth to life.

Thomas Whitbread

NIGHT BEFORE CHRISTMAS

The sea, that great bowl full of jellyfish,
Groaned mutedly beneath the falling snow
And underneath a puff of fallen snow
The beach lay hardened like an ancient wish.

I made a new wish there against the summer,
One suitable to twenty-nine, I thought,
That no new weather coming on unsought
Would find me any colder, any dumber.

Then, when my grief turned stiff and understood
As dead old reindeer in whose eyes ice formed,
I went home, not unwilling to be warmed.
The snow was in me, come what fire would.

Thomas Whitbread

LESSON

Which shell on the beach shall we take home? No matter.
All that shall not fade will be the remembrance
Stirred by the faded shell that all shells shone.

Put the brightest shell into your pocketbook, mother.
Engarland it with seaweedy encumbrance.
Crown the concoction with a glittering stone.

No matter that when we all get home, father
Quite rightly will I-told-you when the shell
Is dull, the seaweed shrunk, the stone but stone.

All laurels crumble, but they are small matter.
The shell and stone plainly remain, and well
Show that the watery flesh dries down to bone.

Thomas Whitbread

CAPE COD IN MARCH

Only the sea looks like summer.
It rollicks its leafy waves,
and turns them. The light
is thin; and the air, chill,
blows too keenly for standing
on the shore, or the windy dunes.
The houses, shuttered, huddled
upon the winter-colored downs,
still cower like silly creatures
who still expect a misfortune
they don't know now won't come.
Everywhere, the dry salt grass
rustles; and the sky, sunny,
pewter, changes as no summer
changes its skies. But the towns
liven. White is being painted
whiter, and people have begun
to move about; the trees along
the little streets are swarmed
with buds, green, scarlet, gray.
In a week or two, forsythia
will shower its peaceful rockets
all over the towns. Meanwhile,
the arm of land lets out
its tiny fleets, trying riggings,
turning the wintry sea
toy-size again. And if gulls
like ancient snow ride motionless
on channels, creeks, edges
of things, robins have come
without persuasion, like
burghers, for the coins of spring.

Robert Wallace

ELEGY FOR FIVE FISHERMEN

Widows of the sea, light many candles,
And forgive us our new voyages,
Our voices loud in the distance
Still talking of profits and fathoms.

Five men drowned on a sunny day,
And a dozen christian towns away
We crown the defeat with another,
Unable, as always, to weep for a mere idea.

For when other men die, from other houses,
We put on solemn faces and we say,
"Tragic but passing, tragic but passing";
And scarcely feel the sudden lurch and sway

Of the long waves as we glide to safe landing—
Scarcely notice the difference at all
Along the torn coast of good fortune
Where we are still standing.

Mary Oliver

INDIAN PIPES

I found them at last, on a hillside
Of laurel and pine, nobbing
From the brown earth with white bowls,
Tender: so wild, so close to home.

The longer I live the more I sense
Wilderness approaching; I used to walk
Miles to find wild things; now they find me,
Blossom under the very windows where
I am busy being grown up and tame.

I think it is more than chance, I think
It is a new kind of vision I have,
That a child, who must put wild things
In a mile by itself, could not bear.
I wake, wrapped in the town, knowing

The edges were only in my mind: all's one.
Indian pipes glisten, inches away.
While patience, charity rub at the cold frontier,
The seeds to everything move in the air.

Mary Oliver

PEAKED HILL BARS

Huge ships once died there, caught upon the rocks
And torn by the white hands of boiling seas.
Their cargoes spilled for miles along the shore.
Drowned men rolled in like barrels to the sand.

Now children, standing in the transient summer,
Stare at the place, and try to understand.
But under the personal heaven of their youth,
The ghost ships they evoke with billowed sail
Sink without terror in the pleasant sea.
Who comprehends the ugliness of truth?
The dark earth turns, and the old landscapes close
Like doors on the rough sound of tragedy.

At Peaked Hill Bars, off Provincetown,
The skin of the wild ocean shines and gleams
And children pause and weave their pretty dreams,
Or hold a ship's bolt or a coin, by chance
Found on the shore—a token saved from time,
Through which disasters whisper like romance.

Mary Oliver

THE SHADOW

Always the one that got away,
That took the bait but broke the thread,
And fathoms underneath us broods
With the weight of the sea above its head,

Always this fish, whose wrinkled sides
Flashed in our arms—this swirling beast
Who fought and finally got away—
This is the one we love the best.

The prizes that our dark hooks tame
Lose their fresh lustre on the scale.
Though we break records with the fish
We catch, the victory grows stale.

The thing we love is miles away.
We had no power to break its pride.
Each time we think of the loose sea
Our minds can see it, magnified.

In our dreams for years to come
It wears our hook within its bone;
Above its shadow we row on
In love with triumphs still unknown.

Mary Oliver

ABOUT THE POETS

Biographical information about most of the poets included in this volume can be obtained from standard reference sources. Of greater importance here is their association with Cape Cod and its influence upon their lives and work.

GEORGE SANTAYANA (1863–1952) taught literature and philosophy at Harvard from 1889 to 1912. During this period he made frequent trips to the Cape. In Volume Two of his autobiography *Persons and Places* he describes a summer picnic in Wareham which inspired the writing of "Cape Cod." "The woods are rather meagre and scrubby in Cape Cod; but there was moss and rock enough by that sluggish little stream to sit down with comfort, and trees high enough to produce the illusion of being embowered. . . . It was on this occasion that I wrote some lines on Cape Cod, of which the poet William Moody said that there for once I had been inspired."

JOSEPH LINCOLN (1870–1944) is the only true "native" Cape Codder included in this volume. Born in Brewster, he was a descendant of a family of sea captains. His intimate knowledge of "Cape Cod folk" enabled him to write over forty books devoted exclusively to the Cape. *Cape Cod Ballads*, from which his poems are taken, was his first published book. During the later part of his life he lived in Villanova, Pennsylvania, but returned each summer to his home in Chatham.

HARRY KEMP (1883–1960) came to Provincetown around 1920 where he lived with his wife, Frances McClernan, in a house called "The Oaks." A large, restless man, he frequently followed his nomadic instinct "riding the rails" or wandering abroad living an open-air, tramping life that earned him the title of "tramp poet." In addition to poetry he wrote novels, social satires and plays which he produced, directed and acted in himself. His last years were spent living alone in a shack on the Provincetown dunes.

CONRAD AIKEN (b. 1889), whose poetry is considered to be one of the major influences in American literature, requested the inclusion of "Mayflower" (Part I) and "The Crystal" (Part

II) in this book because he believes they best exemplify the influence of "Stony Brook" and Cape Cod on his work. He now lives with his wife in a delightful early house in Brewster.

JOHN PEALE BISHOP (1891–1944), West Virginia born author, was associated with Edmund Wilson on the editorial staff of *Vanity Fair* in the 20's. The two men were close friends of Edna St. Vincent Millay and published many of her poems. Mr. Bishop spent summers in Wellfleet, then lived for a short time in South Harwich and in 1937 retired to "Sea Change" in South Chatham where he lived until his death.

EDNA ST. VINCENT MILLAY (1892–1950) spent the summer of 1920 in a "dear little house" called "T'Other Hollow" on Old King's Road in Truro. In a letter to Allan Ross Mac-Dougall she wrote: "It is only a mile and a half to the outside surfy sea, a lonesome beach where you never see anybody but sandpipers. . . . The wind blows a gale about this cottage all the time, and smells so sweet of the little pine woods that is up behind the house, and the hills all around are nothing but overgrown sand-dunes with a bit o'green on, and the sand showing through in bald patches." "Memory of Cape Cod" was written shortly after she returned to the Adirondacks.

EDMUND WILSON (b. 1895) was born in Red Bank, New Jersey and graduated in 1916 from Princeton. His literary career has included managing editor of *Vanity Fair,* associate editorship of the *New Republic,* and book reviewer for the *New Yorker*. Mr. Wilson is known for his social and literary satire and criticism, and most recently, his book of plays *The Duke of Palermo*. He has lived for many years in Wellfleet.

WINFIELD TOWNLEY SCOTT (1910–1968) was literary editor of the Providence *Journal* from 1941 to 1951. A close friend of Charles and Deborah Philbrick, his poem "Thinking of Friends . . ." was written after the summer of 1952 when the two families spent several weeks in neighboring cottages in South Wellfleet. In 1954 he moved to Santa Fe, New Mexico where he lived until his death.

PAUL GOODMAN (b. 1911) is a frequent visitor to Wellfleet. He has achieved recognition as a poet, novelist, dramatist, sociologist, psychologist, community planner and lecturer, and is perhaps best known for his book *Growing Up Absurd*. In his book *Five Years* he writes "From time to time I write a Wordsworthian poem, e.g. on the dunes at Wellfleet, or watching the colorful planes go up. I think I can spell out the conditions that give the Wordsworthian effect. It is a scene where I have no business but to look, as if passing by. It is a scene of a few simple shapes, plain colors, or simple folk, that calms attention. . . . Because the scene is simple and I am personally disengaged, I can describe it with childlike directness."

ELIZABETH BISHOP (b. 1911) grew up in New England and Nova Scotia, and has spent six summers at Wellfleet. In 1949 she served as Consultant in Poetry to the Library of Congress, and in 1956 received the Pulitzer Prize for poetry. Miss Bishop has traveled extensively in Europe and South America. She now lives in Rio de Janeiro and San Francisco.

JOHN HAY (b. 1915) is President of the Cape Cod Museum of Natural History in Brewster. He is author of several books about the natural history of the Cape including *The Run*, *The Great Beach* and *The Sandy Shore*, and is an active conservationist. His forthcoming book *In Defense of Nature* will be published in the fall of 1969 by Atlantic-Little, Brown.

CHARLES EDWARD EATON (b. 1916), a native Southerner, has traveled widely teaching, studying, working and writing. From 1940 to 1942 he served as vice-consul with the U.S. Embassy in Rio de Janeiro. He writes that he and his wife "have spent many happy summers in Wellfleet, and I have done some of my best work there."

AMBROSE GORDON, Jr. (b. 1920) is a professor of English at the University of Texas, but spends as many summers as possible in Wellfleet. His poem "August at Wellfleet," he writes, "was written—or perhaps begun—on the damp edge of Gull Pond during the summer of '56. Mr. Nemerov, with whom I once helped edit *Furioso*, was down the road toward the beach where we went for our noonday swim . . . Paul Goodman came once to swim in Gull Pond."

HOWARD NEMEROV (b. 1920) has published several volumes of poetry as well as four works of fiction and two books of literary criticism and essays. A former Consultant in Poetry at The Library of Congress, he is a member of the National Institute of Arts and Letters and a Fellow in the American Academy of Arts and Sciences. He is currently Professor of English at Brandeis University and has spent summers on the Cape in Wellfleet and Brewster.

RICHARD WILBUR (b. 1921) is a professor of English at Wesleyan University. He has received the National Book Award, a Pulitzer Prize, and several fellowships for his work. He was first exposed to the Cape as a child when he and his parents spent a summer in Brewster. His poem "Wellfleet—The House" was written during the summer of 1948 in a house on the bay side of Wellfleet. Most of his summers today, however, are devoted to Marthas Vineyard. In reviewing his latest book of poems, *Walking To Sleep*, Webster Scott wrote "Wilbur explores emotion, tests its checkpoints and defines the limits of its powers. While the dominant mood of contemporary poetry is an autistic despair, Wilbur directs his imagination to the things that live and the intelligence that hopes."

CHARLES PHILBRICK (b. 1922) is Professor of English at Brown University, specializing in 19th- and 20th-century poetry. He writes "For the last ten years I have spent three months a year on Cape Cod in a house overlooking Blackfish Creek in South Wellfleet. Down-payment on this house was made financially and spiritually possible by the Wallace Stevens Poetry Prize" (which he received in 1958). He has written many Cape poems, a series of which are published in *Wonderstrand Revisited: A Cape Cod Sequence*.

THEODORE ENSLIN (b. 1925) raised cranberries on Cape Cod from 1946 to 1961 when he "retired" to northwestern Maine to "lead a quiet, uncluttered life." Trained as a musician, Mr. Enslin writes "I conceive of all poetry as song, and mine is intended to be read aloud." His poem "Ten Days From Work-In-Progress" is excerpted from the manuscript of a projected long poem tentatively entitled "Synthesis" which, says Mr. Enslin, will probably not be finished within the next ten years. With respect to his poem "9/21/68" he explained "Many of my poems are purposely not titled, since I feel that a name tag without direct relationship to the poem is unnecessary. I have dated a number of poems in this manner, and I feel in this case it conveys the feeling of a September evening."

THOMAS WHITBREAD (b. 1931) first discovered the Cape in 1940 when his parents sent him to Camp Sealore (now Camp Tonset) in Orleans. He is presently Associate Professor of English at the University of Texas, but returns to the Cape every summer. A book of his poems, *Four Infinitives*, was published by Harper & Row in 1964.

ROBERT WALLACE (b. 1932) is Associate Professor of English at Case Western Reserve University. In describing his last book, *Ungainly Things*, Mr. Wallace wrote, "A Poem, if it's any good, is a machine for loving with. It doesn't matter what—the ungainliest thing: a mutt, ourselves, the world. The love depends on the precision." Most of his summers are spent on Marthas Vineyard, and thus "Cape Cod in March" is his only Cape poem.

MARY OLIVER (b. 1935) was born near Cleveland, Ohio and studied at Ohio State University and Vassar College. During the next few years, while living in New York City and England, her poems began appearing in various periodicals. Her first book, *No Voyage and Other Poems*, was published in 1965 by Houghton Mifflin. She now lives in Provincetown where she devotes her time to work at the East End Bookshop and to the writing of her poetry.